FARM ANIMALS

SHEEP

Written by Eliza Nodes

Genius Kid

This edition is published by arrangement with BookLife Publishing

sales@northstareditions.com | 888-417-0195

Library of Congress Control Number:
The Library of Congress Control Number is available on the Library of Congress website.

ISBN
979-8-89471-058-7 (library bound)
979-8-89471-078-5 (paperback)
979-8-89471-116-4 (epub)
979-8-89471-098-3 (hosted ebook)

Printed in the United States of America
Mankato, MN
012026

Written by:
Eliza Nodes

Edited by:
Sadie Hallworth

Designed by:
Ker Ker Lee

Photo Credits – Images courtesy of Shutterstock.com, unless otherwise stated.

Cover – photomaster, carlylyn, bilalwebdesigner, Eric Isselee, mtree555, New Africa, Patryk Kosmider, Patryk Kosmider, Herman Vlad.com. 2–3 – Chris Christophersen, Eric Isselee. 4–5 – Eric Isselee. 6–7 – photomaster, carlylyn, Sarah Marchant. 8–9 – Eric Isselee, silvabom. 10–11 – Eric Isselee, cynoclub, Paul Maguire, Philippe Clement. 12–13 – RR Photo, Ugis Bralens, Andrei Dubadzel, Martins Vanags. 14–15 – Ermak Oksana, Lorenzo Dottorini, mark gusev, New Africa, Alineofcolor, JPC-PROD, bonchan, Aigars Reinholds. 16–17 – Eric Isselee, 3Dimpuls.de. 18–19 – Terelyuk, PeopleImages.com - Yuri A. 20–21 – Steph Couvrette, Nicku, crbellette, New Africa. 22–23 – Roman Samborskyi, photomaster, Eric Isselee, STUDIO DREAM, photomaster.

CONTENTS

Words that look like <u>this</u> can be found in the glossary on page 24.

SHEEP

When you picture a sheep, what do you see?

Do you see a white, woolly fleece coat?
Do you see a sheep being herded by a dog?

Sheep are mammals. They are warm-blooded, have a backbone, and make milk to feed their young.

Sheep are herbivores. They only eat plants. Sheep eat lots of grass.

Some sheep are wild. However, most sheep live on farms. They are domesticated and kept by humans.

DID YOU KNOW?

A group of sheep is called a flock.

BODY OF A SHEEP

A sheep's stomach is split into four parts called compartments. These compartments help it digest all the grass it eats.

Sheep's toes are covered by hooves. Their hooves are cloven, which means they are split into two parts.

DID YOU KNOW?
Animals with four stomach chambers are called ruminants.

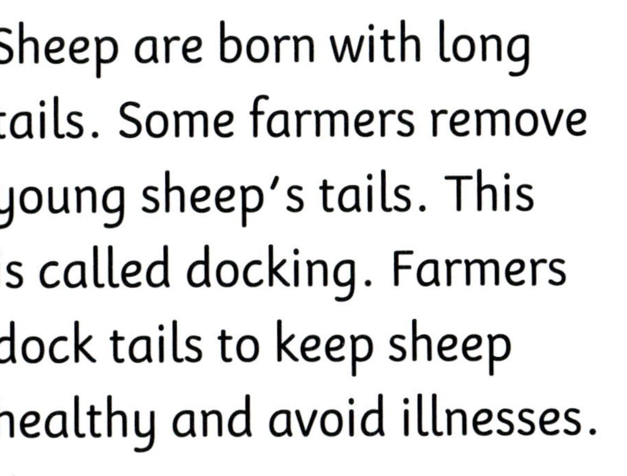

Sheep are born with long tails. Some farmers remove young sheep's tails. This is called docking. Farmers dock tails to keep sheep healthy and avoid illnesses.

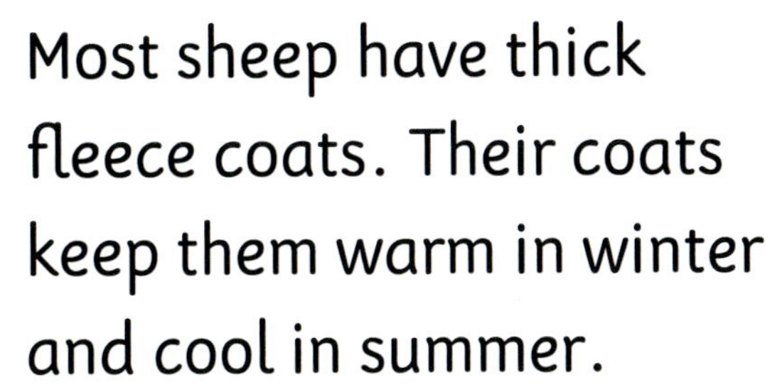

Most sheep have thick fleece coats. Their coats keep them warm in winter and cool in summer.

FACE OF A SHEEP

Some sheep have horns. Sheep horns are made of keratin. Keratin is the same thing human fingernails are made of.

Sheep have an excellent sense of hearing. They can be easily startled by noises.

Sheep's eyes are on the sides of their heads. Their pupils are rectangular. Sheep can see almost everything around them.

Sheep also have a good sense of smell.

All sheep have a small split in their upper lip. This split helps sheep select their favorite plants to eat.

BREEDS OF SHEEP

There are many types of sheep. The different types are called breeds. Humans create breeds by deciding which sheep have young together.

Jacob sheep are white with black spots. Both male and female Jacob sheep have horns. Some of them have up to six horns!

Valais Blacknose sheep have long, white fleece coats and black faces and front knees.

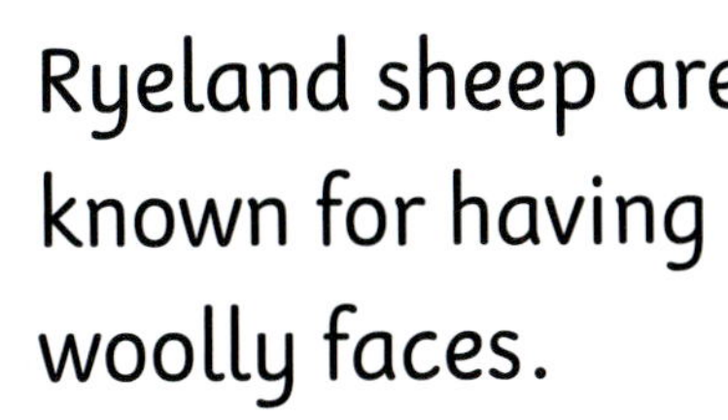

Ryeland sheep are known for having woolly faces.

Cameroon sheep are from West Africa. They have hairy coats instead of woolly fleece coats.

LIFE ON THE FARM

On farms, sheep often spend most of the year outside. Their fleece coats keep them warm.

Some farmers bring their sheep inside barns or sheds during the winter.

While sheep are inside, they are given hay or silage to eat. Silage is grass that has been wrapped in plastic for a month.

Silage

Some sheep eat sheep food made of plants such as corn, oats, and soybean powder.

Sheep food

HOW PEOPLE USE SHEEP

Lamb

Some sheep are made into food.

Meat from adult sheep is called mutton. Meat from sheep that are less than one year old is called lamb.

Lamb kebabs

Mutton

Some farmers keep sheep for their milk. Cheeses such as feta and halloumi are often made from sheep's milk.

Feta

Halloumi

Other farmers use sheep for their wool. Wool can be used to make clothes and blankets.

FROM LAMB TO SHEEP

Male sheep are called rams. Female sheep are called ewes. Baby sheep are called lambs.

Ewes are pregnant for about five months.

Ewes usually give birth once a year, most often in the spring. Farmers call this time the lambing season.

Soon after being born, a lamb's natural instinct to find milk kicks in. The lamb drinks its mother's milk to help it grow.

Sheep can live for 10 to 20 years. Most adult sheep on farms live for around five years.

LOOKING AFTER SHEEP

Like all domestic animals, sheep need to be cared for. Farmers must check on their flocks and make sure they have plenty of food and water.

Sheep need yearly vet checkups. Ewes are checked more often during lambing season.

DID YOU KNOW?
A vet is a doctor for animals.

Farm sheep have their wool removed so they don't get too hot. Removing a sheep's coat is called shearing. Shearing doesn't hurt the sheep.

DID YOU KNOW?

Wild sheep do not need to have their fleece coats removed.

BELIEVE IT OR NOT!

Did you know clones exist? The first adult mammal to be cloned was a sheep named Dolly.

A sheep was one of the first passengers to ride in a hot-air balloon! In 1783, a sheep named Montauciel took flight from France.

People have been keeping sheep for more than 10,000 years.

Have you ever been told to count sheep to help you sleep? Where did this idea come from? Some people think it started with farmers who had to count all their sheep before going to bed.

ARE YOU A GENIUS KID?

Now you know many facts about sheep that will amaze your friends and family. But how much can you remember? Let's find out what you have learned.

Check back through the book if you are not sure.

1. What are sheep horns made of?
2. Name one cheese that is made from sheep's milk.
3. How many times a year do ewes usually give birth?

Answers:
1. keratin
2. feta, halloumi
3. once

GLOSSARY

breeds groups of animals that are bred to have similar characteristics

clones identical copies of a living thing

digest to break down food into things that can be absorbed and used by the body

instinct a natural pattern of behavior in animals

pupils the dark openings in the centers of the eyes that let in light

INDEX